Synæsthesium

Also by Moira Egan:

Botanica arcana (Strange Botany)

Hot Flash Sonnets

Spin

Bar Napkin Sonnets

La seta della cravatta (The Silk of the Tie)

Cleave

Synæsthesium

POEMS

Moira Egan

WINNER OF THE NEW CRITERION POETRY PRIZE

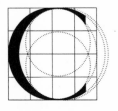

Criterion Books
NEW YORK

*Funding for this year's New Criterion Poetry Prize
has been provided by Joy & Michael Millette*

First American edition published in 2017 by Criterion Books, an imprint
of Encounter Books, an activity of Encounter for Culture and Education,
Inc., a nonprofit, tax-exempt corporation.
www.newcriterion.com/poetryprize

Manufactured in the United States and printed on acid-free paper. The paper
used in this publication meets the minimum requirements of
ANSI/NISO Z39.48–1992 (R 1997) (*Permanence of Paper*).

Library of Congress Cataloging-in-Publication Data

Egan, Moira, 1962– author.
Synæsthesium : poems / Moira Egan.
New York : Criterion Books, [2017]
LCCN 2017034807 | ISBN 9781594039782 (hardcover : acid-free paper)
LCSH: Valadon, Suzanne, 1865-1938–Poetry. | Perfumes–Poetry.
LCC PS3605.G357 A6 2017 | DDC 811/.6–dc23
LC record available at https://lccn.loc.gov/2017034807

Contents

II. *Love and Work: Suzanne Valadon (1865–1938)*

i. *les enfants*

ii. *les portraits de femmes*

Acknowledgments

Deepest gratitude to the editors of the following journals (and anthology) in which the poems first appeared (sometimes in slightly different versions).

Axon: Creative Explorations: "As Sawira," "Casbah," "Cœur de Vétiver Sacré," "Mûre et Musc," and "Spicebomb"

Birmingham Poetry Review: "Love's Baby Soft," "Modèle nu debout et femme nettoyant une baignoire," and "Nu allongé sur un canapé rouge"

Cherry Tree: "Le lancement du filet"

Cordite Poetry Review: "Bouquet de fleurs au napperon brodé"

The Dr. T. J. Eckleburg Review: "Portrait d'Erik Satie" [with thanks, too, for the Pushcart Prize nomination]

Gargoyle: "Baudelaire," "Paestum Rose," and "Lagerfeld for Men"

Hampden-Sydney Poetry Review: "La boîte à violon"

The Hopkins Review: "Lampblack"

The Innisfree Poetry Journal: "Au Lac," "Cuir de Russie," "Magnolia Romana," and "Portrait de Miss Lily Walton"

Literary Matters: "Bois d'Ombrie" and "Maurice Utrillo nu, assis sur un divan"

Measure: "Catherine nue allongée sur un peau de panthère" and "Tabu"

Mount Hope: "Halston Z-14"

The New Criterion: "L'avenir dévoilé ou la tireuse de cartes," "Femme à la contrebasse," "Portrait de famille," "Raminou assis sur une draperie," "Maurice Utrillo, sa grand-mère et son chien," "La chambre bleue," and "Autoportrait." Also, "Baume du Doge"

North Dakota Quarterly: "Shalimar"

Parnassus: Poetry in Review: "Jeune fille faisant du crochet" and "Les œufs de cane"

Poetry Daily: "Lampblack" featured on September 23, 2016

Poetry Northwest: "Adam et Eve"

Poetry Porch: Sonnet Scroll xii: "Catherine nue assise sur une peau de panthère" and "La femme aux bas blancs"

Rise Up Review: "Ce Soir ou Jamais"

The Same: "Nu se coiffant"
So to Speak: A Feminist Journal of Language and Art: "Mira Bai"
      and "Mulâtresse nue tenant une pomme"
Think Journal: "Fillette nue assise sur le sol, les jambes allongées"
Tilt-a-Whirl: "La poupée délaissée" and "Maurice Utrillo enfant,
      nu, debout, jouant du pied avec une cuvette"
The Yale Review: "Jardin du Poète"

The Book of Scented Things: 100 Contemporary Poems about Perfume
      (Literary House Press, 2014): "Mon Parfum Chéri par
      Camille"

Many thanks to the Civitella Ranieri Foundation, where the
Suzanne Valadon series was conceived of and nurtured, and
to the James Merrill House, where many of the "Olfactorium"
poems were written.

And finally, profound and particular gratitude to Damiano
Abeni, Denyse Beaulieu, Heidi Czerwiec, Erica Dawson, Jehanne
Dubrow, Carol Ann Duffy, Rebecca Hecht, Roger Kimball,
Jeannie Marshall, David Yezzi, and, as ever, to my family.

For my mother, Betty Egan

Synæsthesium is the seventeenth winner of the annual New Criterion Poetry Prize. *The New Criterion* is recognized as one of the foremost contemporary venues for poetry that pays close attention to form. Building upon its commitment to serious poetry, *The New Criterion* established this annual prize in 2000.

Synæsthesium

I. Olfactorium

Magnolia Romana

The girl has never seen such plants and trees,
the swaying, pointy cypresses;
the lemons with their shiny, dark green leaves
and fruit as big as fists;
the fragrant basil in the garden near
the lotus pond. Those blossoms, pink
and white, so orderly, mystify her,
how roots can delve so deep in mud. To sink
into it, squelch and play, she longs—another day.
For now she knows to keep her shoes pristine,
the years unsullied,

                         till that white-hot urge
will waft, like sweet magnolia on the breeze.
She'll hold the flowers to her face,
æstival; greedy love nests in the back
of fields or barns, where slivers of sunlight warm
the cedar planks. Forever she'll perceive
the scent of hay as aphrodisiac.

i. Tabu

Love's Baby Soft

"because innocence is sexier than you think"

He's tall and cute, and gestures me to follow
him out the door, spring full-on, lavender
and rose, geraniums exuding pheromones,
a luscious word I'm pleased to have just learned

in 9th grade Bio. "You mind if I smoke?"
He lights up. "Who's that old guy at the bar?"
"My father, who'd'ya think?" "You must be joking."
I shake my head, *I am that poet's daughter.*

And rules are what? He offers me a drag;
I don't. And so he leans in for a kiss,
grown-up and musky, smoky—and then Dad
is there. First time I've ever seen his fists.

Dad sneers at him, "You know she's still a virgin"
and glares at me. I see. It was a question.

Tabu

I wasn't quite a badass yet (in fact
report cards came in, almost always A's;
Behavior: *Excellent*), and yet a crack
(subliminal) was slinking its slow way
toward taking down the perfect girl façade.

Narcissus never had a chance, the mirror
funhoused, not a friend. The books I read
spread-eagled in the fields, wild rose and clover,
would do me, do me in, Totems, Taboos
and Discontents, and Fear of Flying, dusk
transition, homework done, to how I'd use
my body, gleaming, civet, amber, musk.

I ran off to New York, the streets alone,
exotic breezes, neroli and clove.
We woke the morning after, shared an orange.
He wondered why I'd cried. He hadn't known.

Lagerfeld for Men

She isn't in a coma, they insist,
just knocked out: drugs; the booze the night before.
The doctor enters, gleaming, in a mist
of tan suit, bitter orange, and sweet cedar.

It isn't quite the right moment to think
My God this man smells beautiful,
my sister, in the ER, on the brink
of death or something just as horrible.

He sits beside her, takes her hand, and shakes
his head. "I think she'll make it through. However—"
His silence—other lands: vanilla, oak.

       But where are all the windows in this place?
       she wonders as she comes to consciousness.

Years later someone gave some to our father.
My sister and I jolt in shocked recall.
That handsome angel in the hospital.

Halston Z-14

The sidewalk. Bergamot. Adrenaline.
These velvet bastion ropes, though post-heyday
and frayed, might well keep you from getting in.
And will he check I.D.? (You're underage.)
The bouncer doesn't ask. You slip right through.

      A sigh. A breath of cinnamon. A sprig
      of jasmine from the hedge. The powers you—

And there he is, in front of you, gray wig,
arms folded, skinny avatar of cool.
He looks at you, he smiles and tilts his head.
An honor, though they'll give you shit at school

     · (and in nine years this icon will be dead)

because you left with Amber Eyes, whose moss and musk
and leather jacket slung across his shoulder—Lust.

Poison

Eyeliner, shoulder pads, viscose and velvet,
selenotropic mischief, and the grapes
much less of wrath than goth. Concoctions laced
with violaceous liquors, gentian,
vanilla, syrupy, a trace of plum.
We strode the streets, black boots, tight leather skirts,
and biker jackets. Moving violations
and cotton-candy lips. Forbidden fruit.

I'm sure back then I didn't know the root
of *amethyst*: "not drunk," apotropaic
against Excess; nor that the color purple
is named after a mollusk that secretes
a crimson dye (and all the while, that soft,
susceptible creature that's deep within
is mollycoddled by a shell so tough
it lets near nothing pass through. Obdurate.)

ii. Mira Bai

Eau d'Italie

for Ellen

We took the night train, Constance to Florence,
and sat up talking, passed around our sacks
of jellied candies, citron and blackcurrant,
drank Riesling from the bottle, bright green glass
embossed with coats of arms. We crossed the border;
new passengers got on. *Is this seat free?*
He smiled and joined right in, offered us water.
His vaguely musky warmth perfused my sleeve.

All weekend long I sensed him, in a daze
of wine and art and gardens, smooth marble
as white as tuberose. For hours I gazed
at David, willed him off that pedestal
for just one night. That didn't work, of course,
so I set off alone on Sunday, walked
the hills, the yellow clover and the gorse.
Late afternoon, I watched a pigeon hawk
glide effortlessly down. And time to go.

We made it just in time to board our train.
I sat, a lump of clay, beside the window.
A shadow flitted. Someone called my name.
The train was pulling out. I grabbed the lever
to open to him. It was rusted closed.
I saw him say, *I hope you live forever*.

Mira Bai

"I know she was a poet. So am I,"
I tell our bashful driver, who's transgressed
the most important driver boundary:
Don't get too personal, you'll be excessed.

It's not the heat, I think, that paints him rose
from neck to tips of ears. His eyes are deep
as rosewood, fixed, too often, not on the road
but on the mirror, at us, in the backseat.

One afternoon he takes us to a temple
where sandalwood and cedar rise to please
Ma Durga, eight-armed-fierce, yet mother-gentle.
I think he saw the goddess enter me.

The night too hot to sleep. Outside our room
he lights a cigarette; peels peaches, plums.

Paestum Rose

We walked into the restaurant, and steam
(a haze of coriander; sharp, pink pepper)
befogged my glasses so I couldn't see
the man who greeted us. Then—have you ever
become so flustered in the face of beauty
(davana, some strange aphrodisiac)
that your tongue gets stuck, stops functioning completely?
Distracted dinner, wine and furtive looks.

I left my friend alone there. (No, she never
forgave me that, but that's another story.)

He took me back to someone's place (a clever
house-sitter, he? I didn't care). O Lord,
O gusts of incense, Turkish rose, kilims
and pillows, myrrh, O lovely, ancient face.
Love sacred and profane, the last condom.
The candle sputtered, wax on the papyrus.

Ce Soir ou Jamais

A gate, a cloistered garden, stone walls green
with moss and ivy. How can I resist
temptation, this, a chain, a heavy key

ornately wrought of brass? I give a twist
and push my way inside. Bees buzz and croon,
legs thick with pollen, rich the hibiscus

and roses—creamy, damask, "of all hue"
(though there are thorns and brambles here) and blush—
that early-August drooping that exudes

such fragrance, golden, smoldering, a rush
like Poire Williams—and only then do I see
the wooden bench, a man slicing a luscious,

almost-too-juicy pear. *Venez ici.*
He offers me a seat, a wedge of pear.
Perhaps it seems to you a mystery

to find this strange man sitting alone here,
among the insects and the ivory blooms.
I come here for my family, ma grandmère

especially, whose roses, luteous
and beautiful, were envied in the land.
We used to bury jars of unopened buds

and dig them up for dinner parties when
they'd open magically upon our plates.
She was a widow and refused to run,

to leave her home, her garden, when they came.
I feel her spirit here. This is how I pray.

Spicebomb

for Sionna

My sister asks me if I know the name
of that Indian spice-box thing that's handed down
mother to daughter, a sacred legacy.
"In fact, I don't," I say, and sip my tea,
its bergamotty steam transporting me
to Rajasthan, the teeming streets and shouts
and rickshaws zagging through the traffic, cows
and skinny dogs. The markets, where I tried
crisp dumplings filled with broth, the chili's bite,
pink pepper, golden saffron in the rice,
the scent of temples, elemi and fir,
the cinnamon that lingers on the skin.

"Hey, where'd you go just then?" she asks, amused.
"To India—" "Of course. So, was he cute?"
"Oh yes. And always rolled his own, so smelled
of spice and sweet tobacco. —How'd you know
about that spice-box thing? You've never been."

She laughs. "You learn a lot from cooking shows."

As Sawira

for Patrick

Inside the box he's made are precious things:
some sprigs of saffron, oil of davana,
a slotted silver spoon for serving absinthe;
a few dried roses, buds of clove and jasmine.
My memories, he says. *When times were good.*
The box's second shelf holds incense: musk
and labdanum and amber, sandalwood.
*And these are offerings, because I trust
times will be good again.* He's burning oud,
explains it is the potent resin made
when rot and fungus seize the agarwood.

I trace the box's patterns, fine inlay
of figures moving in procession, dark
and light in silhouette. *My family,
or how I would remember them. I carve
these boxes to preserve our legacy.*

It's far too costly for the likes of me.
The box itself is fragrant: cedar, gaiac.
I think of Yeats, his classic saying that
a poem comes right with a pleasing click,
the lid that's fitted perfect to the well-made box.
I say, *Please wrap it for me, carefully*.

Mon Parfum Chéri par Camille

for Denyse

She glides into the room. Her velvet skirts
drag, languid, hem come half undone, a wake
(*there's many a one shall find out all heartache*)
of violet and iris, queer tinctures.

The candles flicker. Lavender shadows
cavort in corners, porphyry to plum.
Our host sees her, greets her with a salaam,
(and *finding that her voice is sweet and low*)

and kisses her, guides her to the window.
He deftly lights her Gauloise, strokes her palm,
her skin not young, but smoothed with years of balm
(because "*to be born woman is to know—*")

She rustles in her bag, pulls out a bottle,
that purple wine whose grape is named for tears,
a stone-walled garden, overgrown for years
(and "*we must labour to be beautiful*").

iii. Jardin des Poètes

Jardin du Poète

The garden's ancient walls are low and broken
and thus (yes, "even at my age") easy
to scale. They say this was a garden Goethe
adored. I see him sketching: helichrysum,
angelica (whose name reminds him of . . .)
and focused: parsing genus, species, love.
I'm sure he knew that cypress is the tree
that marks Italian cemeteries, death
embodied in the dark green spears that gesture
toward heaven. I inhale: crisp vetiver,
grapefruit and orange so pungent that I'm thrust
back to another garden, where I learned
of bitter oxymoron in the sweet
and luscious fruit he fed me, piece by piece;
the faintly musky warmth of his embrace;
the ancient stone walls crumbled, and my trust.

Baudelaire

for JM
(luxe, calme et volupté)

A lazy Sunday morning. The waiter fetches
(complaisant) Bloody Marys made with gin,
not vodka. Glints of juniper and pepper
and wit aglitter spice our conversation.

We have our toast. Whole wheat, and white, and rye—
I do prefer the wry, the poet smiles,
and caraway reminds me . . . faraway
he drifts from us, and stays away, a moment.

And though his neck and wrists are reedy thin,
his shirt's impeccable. *It's Hyacinth*,
he says. *A lovely shade, a dreadful myth*.

We talk of incense, church, papyrus scrolls,
how Sunday morning spent this way is better.
Our waiter's shift is done, he dons his leather,
turns back to us, blows him a kiss farewell.

Baume du Doge

for Mark Strand

In Venice, the *aperitivo*'s garnished
with such voluptuous chunks of orange
that one among us jokes: *Drinks* and *vitamins!*
In truth, though, I recall our conversations,
in equal measure, seriousness and play.
Slow walks and smokes along the Grand Canal,
talk of cinnamon, cardamom, the Spice Trade;
each of us trying to name the precise shade
the sky takes on as the day fades.
Saffron.

He said, *All poetry is formal,*
existing within limits, straits imposed
by language or tradition. Evening knelled in
by San Marco's carillon,
the dusky gusts of myrrh and frankincense.
In a city like this, founded on such elegance,
the silks and velvets trailing wakes of benzoin
and vetiver, the night mind's so sweetly
deceived into believing in permanence.

Bois d'Ombrie

for Seamus Heaney

It could be overwhelming in this room,
so many laurelled heads, their talk replete
with carrots dangled, first names dropped (assumed,
of course, one knows of whom the speaker speaks).
Post-prandial tobacco from the pouch,
tamped into pipes, exhales its sweetly damp
sienna on the air. We take the couch
(he seems to wish to flee his sycophants)
and warm the cognac offered, caramel
and fiery, in tiny crystal glasses.

It's both delicious and medicinal,
I say (who me? say silly things when nervous?).
He sets me right at ease, *Like poetry*
a wee bit, no? Delighting and instructing?
It's hard to hear that lilt and not to think
· of peat smoke rising, umber-black, from chimneys,
and fog as thick as cream on coffee, laced
(delicious and medicinal?) with Jameson.

Casbah

for Galway Kinnell

There is such beauty to be found in darkness,
he told us, so we scribbled in the woods
and underwoods of psyche where he'd led us
to secrets rich and deep, the body's truths,
the body's lies as well, its tattered rags.
Somehow he made us view our selves as sacred,
a kind of incense offered up—nutmeg
and pepper, iris, spiky cedarwood.

One day he found me, sitting in the glade.
I knew he'd read my little cries of pain
(a pane of brittle glass; I was transparent).
He touched my shoulder. *How they must compare
you to the poet J_, such glorious hair.*
He said, *That kind of beauty will not fade*;
spoke kindly of my father, dead for years.

Lampblack

for Cynthia Macdonald

A hurricane knocked out our power once.
Those weeks I read by oil lamp, wrote till late,
and dreamed of Mary Wroth and Dickinson.
The smoke curled up and left a smear of soot.

> (She'd told me that the poets who are blocked
> are those who could not play as children: maimed.
> Too well I know, you can't turn back the clock;
> *ergo*, adulthood full of tricks and games:
> stiletto-skipping down Manhattan's walks
> [*no crack; no break no back*]; encased in latex,
> that orchidaceous, rubbery bouquet;
> the glitter of the night street, glass in asphalt.)

Tonight the sky is black and pepper-crisp.
The moon has never seemed so spherical,
blood-orange or rufous grapefruit, which the eclipse
dissevers, slice by slice, methodical.

Cœur de Vétiver Sacré

for Michael Egan

I've never even found it on a map,
that place he took me to, mystic and strange
in the West of Ireland. Did it start with A?
A mythic name? Arcadia, perhaps?

The very air was green, or so it seemed,
light viridescing through the leaves, from jade
to celadon, from moss to chrysoprase.
We walked and talked beneath the canopy.

He told me that he'd never understood
why my young boyfriend, R_, had disliked him so.
Incredulous: "You don't remember?" "No–"
The drunken phone calls, insults: it wasn't good.

He bowed his head. "I lost entire years,
inflicted damage I can't even name."
"It's all right, Dad, I know, we're much the same
and this place is too beautiful for tears."

We drove in silence, on to Brigid's well,
where pilgrims had left offerings to please:
bright ribbons, incense, careful bricks of peat.
He walked three circles sunwards, prayed for health.

Her elements are water, fire, air.
If he were ashes, I'd scatter him there.

iv. Old Spice

Mûre et Musc

for my mother

Once married, she became an artisan
of ironing. Smoothing, straightening at the seams,
she'd start out with the pillowcases, sheets,
and towels, and even ironed the diapers, bleached
so white they glowed light blue. My mother ironed
for everyone: Grandfather's uniforms;
and Grandma's dresses, for both house and church;
weeknights, our Catholic-school blouses and skirts;
my father's navy trousers, Oxford shirts,
the silky ties he wore only to work.
There's nothing like the smell of laundry, fresh
and soapy-sweet.

            That summer, when he left,
she kept on ironing, holding it together.
It was the summer when the radio
kept her in tears, and him on that jet-plane,
for ever leaving, off into the blue.
The summer of distractions; sleep-aways;
when Skylite snowballs dyed my sister's lips
a terrifying shade of cyanosis.

My mother's favorite color, always: blue.
She loves each shade, cerulean, cornflower,
forget-me-not, and denim, cobalt, true-.
In some parts of the world, one wouldn't dare
to leave the house without a talisman
of blue: blue eye; or lapis lazuli,
that metamorphic rock that's undergone
great transformation, heat- or pressure-borne.

Chantilly

for Grandmother Wolf

She died so long ago, the memories
are few and far between (as she'd have said
herself). A city kitchen, shiny white
and decorated: teapots, china plates
each with a different fruit, strawberry, orange,
and lemon; canisters of different sizes
for flour, sugar, coffee, tea, and spices.
(I do remember she was organized.)

The living room was dark, with furniture
of heavy woods, mahogany and oak,
and always dusted, polished to a gleam.
There was a little garden out back, fenced.
She tended to her roses and carnations,
but in the city air they didn't grow
as much as she'd have liked.

                              We didn't know
her very well, it seems. So when I open
this trunk of things she made—it's a surprise.
The doilies, runners, antimacassars
crocheted in creamy colors, white to pink
to deeper rose, and not a single stitch
is ever dropped (I guess she didn't know
that superstition: always make a glitch
to mollify the jealous gods). And less
of must than of vanilla, that old scent
of something baking, something cleaned,
not fresh exactly. Something rigorous.

Chanel N° 5

for Genevieve Loesch

She bought the house next door, moved in alone.
The neighbors pointed, whispered *Divorcée*
(first time I heard that word). She'd tend her roses,
head held high, shoulders always strong and straight,
in dresses tailored more for town than garden.
My mother was afraid we'd bother her,
our rough-and-tumble chases through backyards
still fenceless then, connected. She cut flowers
and one day brought my mother a bouquet
of iris, lilies: patterned like her dress.

She asked if we could come over for tea.
I heard her tell my mother her great sadness
was she could have no children of her own.
The day arrived. Mom got us neat and clean.
With reverence, we walked into her home,
on to her *parlor*, where she'd laid the tea.

I watched the steam curl up, and smelled a spice
whose name I didn't know. *We'll let it cool
a bit*, she said, showed each of us our place,
a linen napkin, flowered china plate.
At center was a pretty platter full
of tiny cakes in yellow, pink, and green,
a bowl of sugar cubes with silver tongs,
a milk pitcher, a crystal bowl of lemons.
She complimented us, *So elegant*

and beautifully behaved! The afternoon
passed far too quickly, I remember well.

She bent to kiss us each goodbye. Her scent
was powder on the warmth of skin, vanilla.
When we got home, they asked us how it went.
Somebody said, *She must have been a bombshell
in her day.* I didn't know what that meant.
I said, *When I grow up, I want to be
just like her. She's a real lady.*

Old Spice

for Grandfather

My husband rubbed some on as aftershave
one day, then tried to touch me in a way—
I couldn't go there, so, tried to explain:

It is the scent of gentle, of embrace
and sweet vanilla, summer afternoons
of orange juice and the ancient oaky shade
of summer, when he'd set his workshop up
beside the garage, next to Grandma's garden,
the bees, carnations, red geraniums.
He said, *A girl has got to learn to hammer*,
to hit the nail bang on its head, that clang
precise and perfect; he taught me to plane
a plank to silky smooth, the dark cedar
exuding its crisp fragrance as we worked.
Heliotropic, we packed up the tools
and sawhorses when fireflies arrived,
their luminescent lemon signaling
Time to go in, and *Wash up, suppertime.*
Inside, we sprinkled salt and pepper on
the honeydew and cantaloupe. He'd say,
The contrast makes the melon even sweeter.
He'd only stayed in school until 6th grade,
then had to work, but how he loved to read.
At night, he read us fairy tales and Dickens,
and told us of the big book he was reading
about a great white whale.

And just today
I found that chapter about Ambergris.

Émeraude

for Grandmother Selma

She loved to travel, not a trace of fear
of aeroplanes or strangers. "Go, go, go,"
she used to say, her inner flapper, fierce,
coquetting its way out. In old photos,
her smiles are brightest when she's on the road,
bus trips to football games at Notre Dame;
a pony trap from Tralee to Kenmare,
a turf-green blanket spread across her lap.
She even went to Rome to see the Pope.

Sometimes I almost see her, sitting here,
an ornate pew, her head bowed, rosary
fluent between her fingers, incense swirls
ascending, prayers in Latin, mystery.
Glimpses of who she was before the girl
fell ill and died (her only daughter, three).
She'd stayed inside the house for months and cried.

Among the precious things she left behind:
a leather travel wallet, embossed S.H.E.

Bay Rum (Taylor of Old Bond Street)

for Uncle John

When he was young, he spent his years on boats,
the radio man, "Sparky" he was called.
He brought us gifts from everywhere he went:
a family of elephants, polished smooth
of dark, exotic wood; Italian dolls
in local costumes, lime green, ivory, red,
and complicated braids. One year he brought,
for me, a little brooch, a caravel
of finely wrought, bronze-colored filigree.

He brought us stories too, his Chinese wife
and three young children, just like us, a tale
he loved to tell (bald fiction though it was,
and we well knew). He told us of a tree
that grows and grows a hundred years, then blooms,
its flowers white and fragrant. And then dies.

When he retired, he stayed up in his room,
a cabinet of mysteries, old maps
and compasses, binoculars. Each day
he'd take a walk and then a nap, but woke
up happily when we would come to visit.
He let us sniff his cans of coffee, rich
and finely ground; tobacco, damp and sweet,
named for a Swedish lighthouse, Borkum Riff.

He told us, too, how stinky sailors, months
at sea, would rub themselves with fragrant leaves
to smell a little better. Then someone
invented the idea that leaves in rum
and spices would preserve the benefits
so they could even smell good on the ship.

Not long ago, I found the little pin
he gave me. Though it's dark with tarnish, still
it's beautiful, so delicate, and try
though I may, it presents a mystery:
the tiny crimson crosses on its sails
come from a kingdom no one can identify.

Au Lac

for Giuliano and Giuseppina

He's planks and angles; she's all liquid curves,
diaphanous, a water lily floating
(a surface to belie tough roots and nerves
of adamant). He guides her to the boat,
unsteady both, they hold hands on the bow.
Her hair, osmanthus, eddies in the breeze,
freshwater spray. He bends to kiss her, *Now*,
he says, his shyness vanished, as if leaves
of fig and bitter orange could mask the fear.
Her face goes rose, her lips are soft, a bud
just waiting for its blossoming.

                    The years
accrete, seasons of jasmine, cedar wood,
the ancient story traced on brittle pages.
Papyrus lost, shipwreck of memory,
her amber eyes have dimmed, her voice has faded.

She's ever sweet, and every night he weeps.

v. Shalimar

Pure Poison

I only buy white flowers now, jasmine
and tuberose, those blooms that thrive and breed
without the ostentatious color show.
I've found a vintage dress, a talisman,
of palest creamy linen, lace like snow,
and, up the back-side, forty-three buttons
of slightly damaged, artificial pearl.
I'm not sure how I'll button them, but love
the straight-line symmetry. I'm forty-three.

A niece's wedding. Groomsmen, flower girls,
the ornamented, alabaster cake
and toasts proposed, sweet orange juice and champagne;
a soft wind carries blossoms in its wake.
The young ones push me on the dance floor. *No!*
I try to shout, but skitter on high heels.
A sudden, fierce trajectory of bloom—
magnolia flashing, orange blossoms. Boom.
My hand shoots up. I catch the damned bouquet.

Sienne l'Hiver

As children, we were driven, home to home.
I always looked with envy at the lights
that glowed so safe and golden in the windows
against the night sky, darkling to black iris.

Here, now, our window boxes in for winter,
geraniums flaming garnet, tiny violets,
and pale green ferns, as delicate as fingers.
I press my cheek against the freezing glass
and think of what a girl sees from outside.

Woman at window, waiting for her love
to get home, chimney smoke rising. And inside
a fire blazing, sacred woods,
gaiac and olibanum, straw to gold.
A winter stew is bubbling on the stove.

Cuir de Russie

I used to curl up on my west side ledge
and watch the river alchemize from gold
to lead, and spirits sink from hope to dread
as evening, ever earlier, took hold.

The brittle birches with their ghostly white
and spiky branches, waving in controlled
formation with the wind, the anthracite
of winter sky. Their beauty left me cold.

Tonight, years later, I think of those trees
in other ways, the paper white of bark
he peeled to make a Valentine for me;
the smirchy-luscious fragrance of the tar
the Russians used to tan their leather boots.

He comes home, kisses me, then straightaway
goes to the bedroom to take off his shoes.
The cat bee-lines behind him, plays with the laces.
I make us tea with whiskey and some honey
just as the wind kicks up and howls outside.
I say to him, *Old shoe, it's really funny.*
I never thought I'd learn to love the night.

Shalimar

for Damiano

The first notes open harsh, medicinal,
vanilla-Lysol wafting. Cold white halls.

I tell him that its name in Persian means
"abode of love," the gardens where she'd dreamed
in jasmine, lily, lemon, and may rose.
Jahan grieved down those paths, the scent of earth
no comfort to him, Mumtaz dead, in childbirth—
their fourteenth. Then he built the Taj Mahal
for her.

      It was the scent that Frida Kahlo
adored, through both marriages, both divorces.

My husband says, *You smell so good, like Ur-
perfume*. O opoponax, bergamot,
"in sickness, health . . . till death do . . . " yes, he's right.
And love's the orthopedic of the heart.

II. Love and Work: Suzanne Valadon

i. les enfants

Fillette nue assise sur le sol, les jambes allongées (1894)

She hates it when they tell her that her hair
looks pretty that way, and that she should try
to act more like a girl. It isn't fair.

It's not her fault she'd rather run, and climb
the chestnut trees, and chase the boys, and scare
the normal girls, so silly in their fine

white Sunday lace. Already she has plans,
she's not sure what, but she knows she'll escape
this dreary girl-shell life. Look at the hands,

enormous for her size, and fidgeting
as if in practice for piano, or paint.
And with those long, strong, skinny filly legs—

she'll manage. But for now her only wish
is for someone she could tell about the loneliness.

Maurice Utrillo enfant, nu, debout, jouant du pied avec une cuvette (1894)

I want to tell him that I know the ache
he feels, the gnawing emptiness,
like hunger, or a thirst that can't be slaked.

It's difficult, those mornings when he wakes
from hot disordered dreams that mar his rest.
I want to tell him that I know the ache,

the looking glass become a muddy lake
of roots obscured, of pure unknowingness,
of hunger, and a thirst that can't be slaked.

It breaks my heart, the jokes the children make,
that small, angelic face cast down in sadness.
I want to say I understand the ache.

He plays his strange distractions, and I take
some comfort that he's soothing loneliness,
the hunger, and the thirst so hard to slake.

But I can't tell him. Is it a mistake
to hold this secret tightly to my breast?
I want to tell him that I feel the ache,
the hunger, and the thirst that can't be slaked.

Maurice Utrillo nu, assis sur un divan (1895)

*Il faut avoir le courage de regarder le modèle en face
si on veut atteindre l'âme.*
—SV

You have to look a model in the face
to apprehend the soul, you have to delve
down deep for truth, to tell that tale on canvas.
You have to look your model in the face,
no fakes, no kindness; truth a kind of grace.
This skinny little boy, her son, just twelve,
seems helpless in the spotlight of her gaze.
Too young, perhaps, to camouflage his Self,
it's traced in shadows on his tiny face.
It's clear she loves him, draws his awkward grace
with sympathy, his limbs as delicate
and soft as saplings. How can either tell
why he can't look his mother in the face?

Modèle nu debout et femme nettoyant une baignoire (vers 1908)

Those nudes at their toilette,
all pink and warm,
luscious (who put them there like that,
anyway, one might well ask)
limbs outspread, combing
their damp hair, silkily
tangled.

This young lady stands, straight,
elbows angled,
hair pinned up, impatient (*it's cold!
I'm ready!*) as the washer-
woman, bent, scours
and scrubs the bottom
of the tub,

deep zinc vessel with a cross
of joins embossed
on the longer side, a rosette
in the centre. Liminal
the girl stands, waiting,
not quite woman, not child,
a chair

off to the side for when
she's finished with
her bath. Hard and soft, the zinc tub,
warm water, a Turkish towel.

Hard and soft, Degas
said: this is what gives the work
such power.

But isn't it also this:
A glimpse into
the boudoir, chubby maid scrubbing
down the tub, Venus unsure
of how she'll manage
to emerge, graceful,
from this particular
shell.

La poupée délaissée (1921)

She is turning away from the woman, spurning
the matronly touch of soft white Turkish
toweling, she twists, leaning toward the mirror,
left arm the fulcrum, attempting to see clearly
her image there. She's still (surely) a virgin,

plump sweet breasts but little trace yet of the ferny
triangle below the soft belly, nor the yearning
that will find its quenching there.
                         She is turning

at this moment from child to what she's learning,
the crimson duvet cover a voluptuous warning,
the cast-off doll half-on her funeral bier.
Can she see the twinned pink ribbon in her mirror?
(I don't think so.) She is only concerned
with the woman into whom, unknowing and burning,
                         she is turning.

ii. les portraits de femmes

*Il faut avoir le courage de regarder le modèle en face
si l'on veut atteindre l'âme. Ne m'amenez jamais
pour peindre une femme qui cherche l'aimable ou le joli,
je la décevrai tout de suite.*
—Suzanne Valadon

L'avenir dévoilé ou la tireuse de cartes (1912)

The fortune teller clearly has done well,
her lapis satin dress and silver bracelet,
and shiny raven hair tamed in a chignon.

This woman's future isn't hard to tell:
such beauty's never other than an asset,
her tousled ginger braid cascades; her skin

like rosy marble, warmly shimmering.
She's languid on a couch of crimson velvet,
embroidered throws of scarlet, emerald,

and onyx-black; her robe draped just behind.
The fortune teller plucks a card and works it:
This one's the Queen of Diamonds. This one tells,

Mam'selle, of your impending luck, and wealth
of any sort you choose. You will profit
in love, and art . . . (and who knows if, in time, .

the times will catch up with her, incarnate
voluptuousness. Incarnadine.)

Nu se coiffant (vers 1916)

In some other age
she would have been a Magdalene,

that graceful cascade of titian,
the solid body gleaming (and wanton

if you'd need to read
it so). We don't get to see

the features of her face,
just the body's lush profile, traced

from raised elbows bent, arms delicate,
down to curvy breasts, belly, butt,

legs built to bear the weight of an actual woman.
She stands before a deep green curtain

draped in heavy folds,
its surface cross-hatched with threads of gold.

If this were Magdalene,
we'd see her jar of unguent

there, but in this room there's just half a glass
of wine and an open kiss-lock purse,

and a woman who is who she is, whole and bare,
essence and accident, combing her hair.

Mulâtresse nue tenant une pomme (1919)

In the old age, black was not counted fair
—Shakespeare, Sonnet 127

As mistress of this jade glade
and the waterfall behind,

she sits firm, legs slightly crossed,
pressed together just enough

to keep her most private parts
private. The blanket she sits

upon is so white it glows
blue. From the ceramic plate

in front of her—peaches, pears,
plums—she's plucked one ripe apple.

She holds it in her right hand,
weight braced on the strong left arm.

Is this the Great Temptation,
or her way of saying

that any Adam who's stupid
enough to resist this Eve

will likely have an apple
lobbed at his dimwitted head?

Nu allongé sur un canapé rouge (1920)

un beau dessin n'est pas toujours un dessin joli
—André Warnod, *L'Avenir*, Paris

Sometimes one has to draw the line—
not to trace a jumble of textures,
a raw-silk pillow, rough alizarin,
black-satin trimmed, jutting just beyond
the frame of the divan, cherry wood polished
hard and smooth; the heavy red throw
swirling with a forest of embroidery,
black trees, emerald leaves, and spots of sun,
intersected by a lapis slash of velvet,
the peachy-pink upholstery thus veiled,
and scuffed pine planks of the floor

—no, sometimes one has to draw the line
to identify the contours of the nude,
a merciless stroke, precise and firm,
to contain the flesh, sometimes weary,
sometimes soft, but ever lively, ever lovely,
the flow of blood just visible below
the surface, cool and radiant,
the pelvis, smooth belly, breasts that even
sag a bit, and the woman, finally,
complicit, offered up and waiting.

La chambre bleue (1923)

Voluptuous, a luscious word, Delight
and Pleasure stretched out, languid, on the bed,
a silky spread, white flowers on a sky
of turquoise, azure, blending to celeste;
a canopy for privacy, a tent
in which to scintillate the every sense—

but wait. This odalisque is fully dressed:
a peach chemise, pyjama pant striped green
and white, and (*gigolette*!) a cigarette
protruding, brazen, from her lips. It seems
she isn't lying there, a box of sweets
to be consumed. She has her yellow journal,
a crimson-covered book (perhaps Colette?)

Another root of volupté is *will*.

Catherine nue allongée sur une peau de panthère (1923)

Catherine's supine across the panther skin
spread out upon a kilim as in an opium den.
She lies as if post-coital, on the brink,
or sleeping, unaware she might be posing,
her any secrets kept behind closed eyes.
Her breasts seem near immune to gravity,
the flesh pulled taut from ribs to abdomen,
that pleasing angle whence to view a woman.
Perhaps we're meant to think she's had some wine
(perhaps, even, too much), and yet her thighs
stay pressed together decorously, feet
relaxed, and from this angle we can see
the foot's fine arch, the calluses from the street—
the splendid paradoxes of Catherine.

Catherine nue assise sur une peau de panthère (1923)

Catherine relaxes on the panther skin
that's draped across a chair as in someone's den.
She's off in thought, or maybe on the brink
of boredom, ready to return to posing,
amusèd resignation in her eyes.
Her breasts point downward; clearly gravity
is not a stranger, and her abdomen
protrudes, a friendly paunch, here is a woman
who probably enjoys her cheese and wine,
and why not? She works hard—look at those thighs,
their massive strength, and yet the lovely feet—
aristocratic promise gone unseen
by anyone she passes in the street.
To them she's just the charwoman, Catherine.

La femme aux bas blancs (1924)

If *he* had painted her, I fear she'd be
a succubus—not succulent and rare,
plopped solid, rightful on the Empire chair,
hands clasped casually, propping the right knee
across the left, allowing us to see
a swath of healthy thigh, skin smooth and fair,
between white stockings and lace-edged underwear
that peeks out from beneath the red chemise.

She doesn't seem even to have the time
to kick off those *Louis Quatorze* heels,
stage makeup still intact, the contoured eyes
and carmine lips emphatically defined
by a practiced hand. She'll not say what she feels
about the abandoned, showgirl-rose bouquet.

iii. l'art

iii. l'art

Jeune fille faisant du crochet (vers 1892)

If not for the orange ribbon in her hair,
she might be a novitiate at prayer,
head bent in concentration, eyes intent
upon the single sepia filament
of wool or silk, her needle flashing, bright.
The gauzy curtains shimmer, featherlight,
blown inward by a gentle breeze, as if
a gesture of the breath of inspiration.

But she sits, solid, still, oblivious
to anything that's not her work: her dress
perhaps a little scratchy, her black smock
too heavy, and the chair, its creaks and cracks.
This moment, all she knows, her yarn is soft
and fine, and from it, she creates her cloth.

Femme à la contrebasse (1914–15)

How much more angled could this parlor be?
With olive walls stolid, and frame upon frame
of a window, glass leaded, just over a mantel
of onyx and ivory, which bevels from yellow
to flame.

She, on the other hand, curve against curve,
is a woman who plays double bass.
Is she out of proportion to show the importance
of elegant fingers and wrists that are strong?
The bass bends its waist to her, posing and poised,
her own face a study in wide-eyed and wonder.

And what will you do with this, viewer,
with this new confusion of music, of muse
and of mistress, when she to be played upon's
suddenly player, and she to be painted,
her skin for the offering, walks round the easel
with ease, becoming the painter?

La boîte à violon (1923)

Desktop covered, beautiful jumble: tulips
cut, arranged with care in the ocher
pitcher. Next the "drapery with the eyes," its
                    serpenty patterns,

red and blue embroidery on the linen
falls beside the amphora-shaped Chinese vase,
blues and greens worked cunningly to create a
                    porcelain landscape.

Supple muscles, seemingly frescoed, casting
nets behind, with malachite-shaded contours.
(Here the artist craftily says, *I know just
                    what I am doing*.)

Cobalt vase glows next to the tiny paper-
back, a volume yellowed, dog-eared, beloved.
Finally, the violin on its red swirls,
                    cosseting velvet,

bow and neck slant parallel, but the center
here is clear: the feminine curve, the fiddle's
haunting human womanly voice: the vibrant
                    act of creation.

L'aide amicale aux artistes: Bal de l'AAAA au Gymnase municipal (1927)

Delacroix's *Liberté* guides
her people across the *champ
de bataille*, right arm aloft,
tricolore grasped in that hand,
a musket in the other.
Bare-breasted, near-Boadicean,
she strides among the corpses,
glancing back only to see
that her compatriots are
right behind: *Égalité*,
Fraternité. And that young
boy who looks elsewhere, wielding
two pistols. Sulfurous smoke
obscures buildings and blue sky.

Even on a gray November day, one can
catch a whiff of jasmine. Imagine instead,
vue de derrière, muscles and curves, a nude,
right arm aloft, paintbrush inscribing flowers:
roses incarnadine, irises forget-
me-not blue, wisteria blending all hues.
In her left hand she holds a palette, thick daubs
of white, blue, red, yellow, and green. This is not
a dream (gold coins tumbling onto the platform,
the floor) but a placard for a Friday night,
20th of May, 1927,

"*l'aide amicale aux artistes*," each one reaching
his or her arm out to support another.

14 novembre, 2015

Bouquet de fleurs au napperon brodé (1930)

The come-hither hibiscus aims its pistil
straight at your face, petals outspread
in invitation. You can almost catch
the roses' heady scent, their variations
from palest pink to scarlet and carnelian,
the blush that blooms along the lover's throat.
Gladiolus gestures up; lilac and heather
(just for contrast) stand erect and azure.

Even the spout points out at you,
revealing the side on which the lines
conjoin, wedding night mehndi
or the V of a woman's upper thighs.
And the table-mat, gorgeously embroidered,
looks morning-after rumpled; its white
directs the eye to the cupboard behind.
What vibrant stories might be locked inside?

Les œufs de cane (1931)

Round
and flat,
domestic
with a touch of wild:
a basket of duck eggs, rustic
yet deliciously
balanced, straw
bed on
which

they're
further
cosseted,
chiaroscuroed,
bright lead white mottled green and gray,
the basket's handle
casting dark
ovoid
shade.

Each
still life
speaks volumes
of the artist's life
out of which it arises, work
and passion balanced;
ardour, care,
eggs in
one

brown
basket
because this
is all that matters:
fertility, flavor in all
their forms, walls and floors
firm supports,
cool and
tiled.

iv. la famille

Maurice Utrillo, sa grand-mère et son chien (1910)

He's learned to look into his mother's eyes
and gazes straight with equal parts chagrin
and love, the drunken nights no more surprise

to her. He holds his left hand angled, strong and fine;
his face is pale, his beard Mephistophelian.
(What deal's been struck with whom, and at what price?)

Grandmother, meanwhile, looks off to the side
and downward, face etched, permafrost, the frown
she nearly always wears (despite their life

if not of luxury, at least of pride).
Her life's work, too, shows clearly in her hands.
She managed to escape the village gibes

and get to Paris. Why then can't she smile?
Her daughter, lovely, could've had any man
she wanted (and she did). The boy's profile—

one has one's theories. Yes, the girl was wild.
But family is family: mother, son,
grandmother—even some love set aside

to lavish on the dog, with gentle eyes
and paw outstretched beside Grandmother's hand.

Portrait de famille (1912)

Clockwise, from top left:

André
The perfect skin, his hair and beard close-trimmed,
his suit and tie impeccable. He takes
such obvious care
of himself and others, ever tries to make
it all respectable. Stands a bit distant.

Maman
We're fairly certain that she hasn't smiled
in thirty years. There must have been
one night (beguiled? beguiling?). Her lips sealed,
not just turned down in that eternal frown
but also signed in silence.

Maurice
It's said that melancholy often skips
a generation. Dear boy, heavy head,
rests heavy on his hand, elbow on knee.
It's all too clear, he'd really rather be
(anywhere else) at the boîte, even his easel.

Suzanne

At center, right hand at the heart,
and fingers spread apart, between the breasts.
The gaze is straight and clear, a bit ironic.
At center, yes, and holding all intact.
If these are family bonds, they are ionic.

Maurice Utrillo devant son chevalet (1919)

As if to savor these moments of peace
when he sits, forward, focused, at his easel,
a half-smile playing on his face,

as if to erase the smashed glasses, the tantrums,
the admissions, the releases, the asylums,
the promises kept until the first sip of wine—

They say it was the painting saved his life.
But even in the quiet
of his studio, do you sense the anxiety?

The wall behind's the shade of Beaujolais
and the angles of the frames and table seem to paint
him into the corner of his own, sad making.

The rough strokes and the jaundiced
palette beg the eternal question
of just how much a mother can do for her son.

Raminou assis sur une draperie (1920)

There are certain disadvantages
to being an artist's cat: you can't,
for example, jump into the lap
of a model who's naked, even
if the studio is cold; you can't
expect the scratch behind the ears when
she's painting, and though she leaves the food
down for you, sometimes you can't touch her
for hours because she's lost in her work.

And you must be careful with your claws
so you don't ruin her props: the fine
silk; filmy cotton; and that strange one
that looks back at you with haunted eyes.
You can't play like a normal cat; trap
mice in corners; make noise at midnight;
mewl at the moon. But then, after all,
an Egyptian goddess on a swirl
of soft fabrics, you're made immortal.

Portrait de Miss Lily Walton (1922)

Miss Lily Walton sits
composed on the Empire chair,
her day's work over.

Miss Lily Walton takes
pride in her work,
the clever arrangements:
a house plant between
an extravagant doll
and the painted oval box,
the dust-free sheen
of the marble sideboard,
and the curtain
draped gracefully down.

Miss Lily Walton, in
her starched white blouse
plain black jumper
and very sensible shoes,
is almost a part
of the family. And after all,
England is not that far.

Miss Lily Walton, with
silver-red hair pinned up
and eyes of intelligent blue,
looks quite comfortable
holding the family's
favorite cat, the prepossessing
ginger, Raminou.

v. l'amour

Portrait d'Erik Satie (1892–93)

How to love a younger man:
look deep into each other's eyes, cyan.
Then show him what to do with his hands,

so eloquent
on that other instrument,
but totally unpracticed on a woman.

Praise
his eccentricities,
the waxed moustache, the *pince-nez*,

his top hat
and his constant costume of black.
Make it clear you understand that

his surface is just his visible core,
and that his mark on the world
will be indelible.

Suffuse each kiss
on those full red lips
(almost womanly in their voluptuousness)

with all the tenderness of knowing,
already, that when you go,
you will leave him with such sorrow,

with *nothing but an icy loneliness*
that fills the head with emptiness
and the heart with sadness.

(The italicized portion is from Satie's letter of March
11, 1893.)

Le lancement du filet (1914)

He swings back, *contrapposto*, and the muscles
ripple like salmon swimming, ardent flesh
contouring in sinewy lines, supple

and smooth. He turns, arms outstretched,
and looped around his forearm is the puzzle
of strong silks woven into mesh.

He turns again, thighs taut, full frontal
(and the fig leaf here is the net)
astride two rocks, his left elbow

bent, wrist to chest, right arm extended
in an attitude Nijinsky might have invented.

Adam et Eve (1909)

The man and the woman
are simply part of this garden

in which there is no serpent
lurking.

They *gavotte* or *pavane*
across the lush of emerald green

and the ferrous brown of fertile
earth.

Everything's alive
and intertwined, the vines,

the sky's cerulean
reflected in their skin,

the leaves and limbs
of the trees; the two, arm in arm.

Ripe fruit hangs,
carmine and yellow, yin and yang

and the one she chooses,
unblemished, unbruised,

seems more a fruit of promise
than of dark, forbidden knowledge.

His fingers
softly wind around her wrist

in a gesture that's much less
no than *yes*.

André Utter, nu de face (vers 1909)

One wonders if they had an argument
the night before, his head cast down,
his features blurred, as if he is intent
on keeping what's inside inside,

which is, perhaps, the thought that she's the better,
the masterful one, pencil, paint.
Who will recall the name, André Utter,
except as love and subject of

Suzanne? "Suzanne the Terrible": they clash
sometimes, the wine, the son, the years
that separate them. But then, both, abashed,
sink warmly in each other's arms,

as here, he stands, full-frontal, no defense,
his legs well-muscled, yet something
about the shoulders, arms, conveys a sense
of softness, longing for embrace.

He steps down from the pedestal,
and walks toward her. *It isn't that we fight
(for every couple does, you know);
it's how we learn, in love, to make it right.*

Autoportrait (1927)

This mirror tells no lie. She's sad and tired,
and every corner of her being's drawn
down, the earthward tilt of cobalt eyes,
lips pressed together in a jaded frown;
the shoulders slump a bit, her neck's the creased
axis that supports the heavy head,
and flesh is mottled, modeled cool and green
and lavender and blue, a zag of red
across one cheek (*en colère?*), orange and rust,
the cinnabar of curtain, drooping leaves
in faded jade, and apples, red and mustard,
autumnal, long since fallen from the tree.

This is the toll of love and gravity.
And yet you cannot disregard the beauty.